This book is dedicated to the future generations, including my own children, Harlen and Jasper, who rely on changes being made to our current practices to secure a healthy environment for the future.

Kimberly Joyce Koyczan

PLASTIC: THE SIDE DISH YOU GET WITH EVERY MEAL

AUSTIN MACAULEY PUBLISHERS

LONDON * CAMBRIDGE * NEW YORK * SHARJAH

Ordering Information
Quantity sales: Special discounts are available on quantity purchases by corporations, associations, and others. For details, contact the publisher at the address below.

Publisher's Cataloging-in-Publication data
Koyczan, Kimberly Joyce
Plastic: The Side Dish You Get with Every Meal

ISBN 9798889109068 (Paperback)
ISBN 9798889109075 (ePub e-book)

Library of Congress Control Number: 2024922622

www.austinmacauley.com/us

First Published 2025
Austin Macauley Publishers LLC
40 Wall Street, 33rd Floor, Suite 3302
New York, NY 10005
USA

mail-usa@austinmacauley.com
+1 (646) 5125767

I would like to acknowledge and thank The Guardian News for continuing to publish research articles on microplastics, and its effects on animals, and the human body. The Guardian News has published breakthrough information regarding microplastics in the environment and how its tremendous presence in landfills and in the food chain is a risk for human health. I would also like to thank all the great work done by researchers and scientists who continue to study how microplastics impact human health, as well as the innovators working on finding alternative solutions for the harmful products we use today. Without brilliant contributions like these, this book would not have been possible. I would like to encourage all future generations, and young people to continue raising concerns on current global issues like climate change in hopes for a better, more sustainable future and healthier planet. I'd like to extend gratitude to my two children, Harlen and Jasper, for motivating me to work hard towards positive changes in all areas of my life, while sharing the same passion and appreciation for the land we live on, and all its inhabitants. Nature is beautiful.

Table of Contents

Abstract

With this piece of writing, I would like to call to attention to the crisis of contamination related to the global use of plastic products and packaging. At any given time, you can find everyday items that are made of plastic. It's astonishing how little data has been collected or researched so far, on a product that we as humans have mass produced, and incorporated in our daily lives without knowing how it may impact our health. The topics I wish to explore are: to what extent has the use of plastic items and the garbage accumulated from them has impacted the environment; how the continued use of these products has impacted human health; and options for new products to replace environmentally harmful products moving forward. I would like to explore what causes microplastic exposure in humans, wildlife, and the environment. What environments create the greatest risks for exposure, which wildlife species have been most affected, and to expose recent findings of the impacts caused by the heavy use of plastic products, and how we are exposed to microplastics in our daily lives. Taking a detailed look into the most common consumer products that cause microplastic ingestion in humans with focus on an alternative option for consumer products moving forward, that will greatly reduce the continuous flow of plastic and harmful emissions of other materials into the landfills, atmosphere and natural ecosystems. A review of what products do the most harm to the environment during construction & building maintenance; how an alternative product can replace plastic, putting an end to the cycle of how consumer products are currently harming the environment while reducing impacts of climate change and world contamination by implementing its use. Fish and water organisms have no choice but to take in microplastic and chemical pollution present in their habitats. I wish to speak up for those who do not have a voice to defend themselves, like the plant, fish and wildlife communities that are most affected by plastic waste, industrial and agricultural pollution. It is naive to think that this issue stops at the landfills or in the oceans; the reality is that it has impacted every organism and every ecosystem on Earth. How does it affect the food on our plate? And what can we do to change this?

Introduction

Some of the most common household items, food and drinks, the air we breathe, and lengthy time spent indoors, could all be putting your health at risk. One of the most common materials that we use in our everyday lives is plastic. Plastic is everywhere; we use it to package and eat our food, with disposable cups, plates, and cutlery, serving trays, water bottles, and tin foil. Plastic is used as packaging for most consumer goods, such as shampoos, body wash, dish soap and laundry detergent bottles. We use it in our homes every day to wrap food, and store items in plastic bins and containers. Over the past 60 years, the human population has generated about 8.3 billion tons of plastic waste, and about 12 million tons of it ends up in the World's oceans every year. This book will explore how microplastics enter the environment, the impacts of microplastics on environmental and human health, how microplastics enter the digestive system and blood of living organisms, what environments are at highest risk for exposure, and how the average person can take steps towards minimizing their exposure for inhalation and ingestion of microplastics. It will focus on alternative products that can replace the use of plastic and other harmful products used in common practices worldwide, with hope for a more sustainable, less toxic future for the planet, and all beings.

Thesis statement: The accumulation of plastic waste generated by the human population has become so extensive that it has entered our food chain, and contaminated the air we breathe. More research must be conducted to determine how this will affect our health in the future, proposing a solution that will prevent further environmental damage, by changing the current materials of manufactured consumer products.

Chapter 1
From Plastic to Microplastics

The heavy use of plastic products by people is mainly due to their convenience, lightweight nature, water resistance, and reasonable price. People tend to prefer convenient items, such as using plastic cutlery instead of washing dishes and opting for quick take-out meals instead of cooking As a result, discarded food containers and take-out packaging accumulate rapidly in this fast paced world.

Photo Credit: IMSD International Master in Sustainable Development and corporate responsibility. IMSD International Master in Sustainable Development and Corporate Responsibility RSS. (n.d.). Retrieved May 5, 2023, from https://www.eoi.es/blogs/imsd/dp-2-food-waste-in-gastronomy-industry/

The societal use of plastic products continues to feed the crisis of global accumulation of plastic waste, and raises concerns about how contamination might affect environmental and human health. As plastic continues to endlessly flow into our landfills and accumulate, environmental factors like UV radiation, oxidation, and mechanical effects cause these plastic materials to break down into smaller particles called microplastics. Microplastics are considered as any particle of synthetic plastic smaller than 5mm, which allows it to transport more easily to surrounding environments (22). The small size of microplastics allows them to easily transport through the environment, not only by leaching through soils at landfill sites, but they become airborne which results in inhalation of microplastics by humans, and wildlife. As microplastics travel through various environmental systems, they tend to pick up and attach to other toxins, which get carried along with them as they continue to disburse to surrounding areas. Microplastics continue to break down into smaller particles called nano-plastics, which are small and hard to detect. They are so hard to detect in fact, that it may cause their presence in the environment to be overlooked. However, just because something can no longer be seen or detected does not mean that it is no longer there! *Wasser 3.0., Microplastics, (2022)*. In 1950, the world's plastic production was 1.5 million tons, which increased to 348 million metric tons by 2017. Larger pieces of plastic from landfills flake off, and degrade into microplastics, which then leach into the surrounding environments transported by water sources into soils, land vegetation, and the ecosystems of marine organisms (23). There are two types of primary microplastics, Type A regards microplastics as a chemical; these Type A microplastics are directly added into cleaning solutions and personal hygiene products. This additive is then replaced by water soluble polymers, which are just a liquid version of microplastics. This fine alteration results in companies claiming that their products are "free from microplastics" (22). Plastic pellets are used in products like face wash, moisturizers, cosmetics, and shaving products; which then get washed down the drain, where it enters the environment (23). Type B, are microplastics that are released to the environment from the use of other plastic products. For example, when we use plastic cups, dishes, and storage containers, plastic flakes off into the surrounding environment, and into the food and beverages they hold (18). Another example of Type B microplastics, are the fibers produced from tire abrasion on roads (18 and 22). Secondary microplastics are formed in the environment resulting from the decay of larger pieces of plastic, this process is influenced by UV radiation, bacteria, and friction. Plastic takes a long time to decay, doesn't break down easily, and has the ability to remain in the environment for lengthy periods of time. Microplastics are often transported through ocean currents and distributed into the environment (22). Depending on the composition of the plastic material will determine the rate at which it breaks down and distributes into water, air, and soil. (1).

Chapter 2
Microplastics and Soil

The cause for microplastics being found in soil is a result from larger pieces of plastic degrading into smaller particles that leach into the soils close to landfill sites. Environmental factors, like seasonal changes, and high temperatures, assist in the breakdown of plastic products in the environment. Another way that microplastics make their way into soil is by getting discharged from sewage treatment plants, and industrial waste water systems. Microplastics have the ability to leach from soil to water; when plastic from landfills flow into rivers, streams and oceans. Conversely, they can also leach from water to soil, when plastic from the ocean leaches into soils and vegetation that border water sources. Soil has the potential to be a reservoir for microplastics, where they can accumulate over long periods of time. Soils are referred to as a carbon sink that stores carbon until the soils become disrupted, releasing carbon into the atmosphere. When plastic begins to break down in landfills, some of the plastic fibers become airborne. As microplastics travel through the environment, assisted by the natural functions of ecosystems, they bind with environmental pollutants, which then get carried with them to wherever they settle. This causes direct contamination and toxicity to the environment and the organisms that come into contact with them. Microplastics cause chemical changes in soil, which affects the growth and performance of plants, surface vegetation, and soil organisms. The way that microplastics in soil could possibly affect human health, is that microplastics from landfills have been detected in agricultural soils, and mulch, which is used to grow food for human consumption. Additionally, landfills contribute to airborne microplastics, demonstrating that after plastic breaks down into smaller pieces, it can literally disburse into every known environment on Earth. During a study, ten soil samples were collected from a landfill site in Bangladesh from different depths, three of the soil samples contained microplastics. It is very difficult to detect microplastics because of their small size, and detection requires thorough examination with proper equipment, but can still be easily overlooked (1). Another factor to consider for microplastic contamination in soil is that gardening soil is sold in plastic packaging, then sits out in a garden center exposed to UV rays from the sun, resulting in plastic leaching into the soil. Then we use this soil to plant vegetables for personal consumption.

We believe that growing our own food is healthier for us, but it can potentially create health risks due to microplastics that are already present in soil or that leach into the soil we use for cultivation. Additionally, there is a risk of contamination from the water we drink and water our plants with. It is important to note that contamination can also come from natural sources, through evaporation and precipitation, where airborne contaminants settle on vegetation, soils, and open water sources that wildlife rely on for food and survival.

This is also true for other harmful pollutants that are produced during road construction, building demolition, maintenance, heating, and operation of structures. We can make the link between animals that consume forest vegetation grown from contaminated soils near the roadside or by consuming plants where pollutants have settled on the surface of leaves. Through my studies in renewable resource management, I have learned that this concern is greater in Northern regions because heat, smog, and pollutants rise into the atmosphere and settle to the ground once they enter colder climates. However, at the current rate that plastic waste is produced every day, there is no region on Earth that is excluded, safe, or exempt from microplastic contamination. It is important not to be misled into believing that this is an issue specific to Arctic and Northern regions because it is a global problem. Expanding on the issue of contaminated soils, and vegetation, these added risks interfere with cultural practices which include harvesting wild game, fish, berries, and medicines from the land. The importance of healthy soils is essential to supporting life and relies heavily on soil organisms that play an essential role contributing to the nutrient richness and porosity of soils. The more we claim natural, untouched land and convert it into commercial developments, residential properties, and roadways the more we inevitably doom ourselves along with many other wildlife species. Excessive expansion into these areas deteriorates Earth's most lush organic layer, which is essential for food production, supporting trees, and plants that produce oxygen, basically supporting all life on this planet.

Chapter 3
How Microplastics and
Other Man-Made Products Impact Wildlife

The wildlife species that are most heavily impacted by plastic waste in the environment are marine organisms, and birds. The most common types of plastic consumed by marine life are fishing nets, ropes, styrofoam, and plastic bags. Plastic in the oceans has caused the deaths of countless seabirds, sea mammals, and fish. When pieces of plastic are picked up by sea currents, light is reflected off the plastic particles, which makes them shimmer in the water. This is what causes marine animals to confuse plastic with food, because it looks like a shiny fish or plankton, which is a common food source for these species. When animals and birds eat plastic found in the environment, they get a false sense of fullness with no nutritional value, which results in death from malnutrition. One study conducted by Japanese researchers discovered flame retardant in the tissues of seabirds, which was directly linked to swallowed plastic (23). In Brazil, autopsies were done on 371 Leatherback turtles, and 37% of them had plastic in their bodies; floating plastic that resembled jellyfish was the cause for ingestion. One hundred, and ten birds from 10 different species were also tested, 64% of them had plastic in their stomachs. The types of plastics that were recovered from their stomachs consisted of: 35% plastic pellets found in personal hygiene products, for example the microbeads found in face & body wash, and 62% of it was plastic container fragments (23). Chemicals that are added to plastic during manufacturing have been linked to reproductive, and developmental issues in marine species, impacting their populations. Deep ocean crustaceans were examined, and not only did they have plastic in their bodies but also fibers from synthetic clothing. Swedish scientists conducted tests that revealed that microplastics have the ability to enter the brains of fish, causing abnormal behavior. When an organism has ingested microplastics, the contamination can transfer up the food chain through predator-prey relationships; this process is called trophic transfer. Chemicals have the ability to leak from plastic, even when it is inside the body of an animal (17). Some tests conducted on animals showed cell shutdown, inflammation, and metabolic issues as a result from microplastic contamination in the body (13). Microplastic bioaccumulation in wildlife species can be transferred to humans through wild game animals that are hunted as a food source. Every ecosystem on Earth is linked to one another. This isn't just an issue for the most recent Harbor seal that died of strangulation by a drift net; this issue is a concern for everyone and everything on Earth.

Chapter 4
One Person's Trash Is a Bowerbirds Treasure

Another concerning issue with so much garbage floating around in the environment is that some avian species, like Satin Bowerbirds, have been greatly affected by plastic waste. They have a very peculiar mating ritual that involves the male building a bower, which is a ground nest that resembles a little house made of sticks and grass. Then, collects as many treasures and shiny objects as he can find to decorate the bower to attract a female. A big collection of attractive objects is impressive to the female Bowerbird, and selecting a mate is based on how well the male builds his bower, This demonstrates his ability to go out and collect fancy items to decorate his bower, and avoid predation while doing so. Historically, favorable decor for a bower included flowers, feathers, shells or leaves. However, rapid accumulation of waste had Bowerbirds take a liking to the color blue. They began decorating their bowers with bottle rings, caps, and other plastic items, which can have a fatal consequence if they get entangled. Even the small plastic ring around milk jugs can result in death for these little builders (27).

Photo Credit: Siossian, E. (2018, October 5). *Satin Bowerbirds do a risky dance with plastic waste*. ABC News. Retrieved May 5, 2023, from https://www.abc.net.au/news/2018-10-06/satin-bowerbirds-falling-victim-to-plastic-waste/10215078

Most avian species have resulted in building nests lined with trash, most of it being plastic. A recent study has led to a diagnosis of a new disease in shorebirds called plasticosis, which is a direct result from ingesting plastic. This ingestion causes inflammation, damage to the digestive tract, preventing nutrient absorption, scarring from the inability to digest plastic waste, and lowered immunity to parasites and infection. The presence of plastic debris in the environment has led to a decline in bird populations from birds feed their offspring fragments of garbage, resulting in starvation for both young and mature birds. Unfortunately, there is an abundance of plastic readily available for ingestion (5). Another concern for wildlife and avian species is the contamination of wetlands, lakes, and rivers by lead shots, ammunition, and fishing lures made with lead. Discarded ammunition sitting at the bottom of water sources creates lead contamination. Wildlife species, especially waterfowl, ingest some of the lead shots, leading to lead poisoning. Additional concern for pollutants are abandoned tires discarded into water sources from illegal dumping. Another impact caused by lead shots is that when used for wild game hunting, the animal usually doesn't die immediately after being shot. As a result, lead from the ammunition has entered the blood system of the animal, and circulates through its body as the animal takes its last breaths. Wild game is harvested for consumption after being killed with lead shots, which poses a risk to people because lead fragments can be present in meat and blood of the animal, which can transfer to individuals that consume the meat. However, there have been suggestions regarding proposed materials for green ammunition that does not contain lead. This would eliminate the risk for lead poisoning, and potential kidney disease caused by consuming wild meat that was harvested with a lead shot. Green ammunition is a way to make wild meat safer for consumption, removing heavy metals from bullets, that will reduce contamination, and ozone depletion caused by toxic substances used in commonly sold ammunition cartridges (8). Lead contamination in wild game can also pose a risk to bone density for those who consume the meat. Additionally, it is riskier for women regarding future pregnancies after regular consumption of contaminated meat. Lead exposure during pregnancy can affect the unborn baby leading to developmental issues down the line like attention disorders, and behavior problems. Lead contamination remains in the body for a while after consumption and elevates the presence of lead in the blood system, however, the levels of lead present in blood will decrease after using ammunition that does not contain lead (25).

Chapter 5
Causes for Microplastic Exposure in Humans

Although the accumulation of plastic in our landfills is concerning, the greatest risk of exposure to microplastics is found in your own home, where people spend most of their time. The ability of microplastics to leach from surfaces into food and beverages, as well as being directly present in some food items and tap water, is a direct source of microplastic ingestion by humans. "People spend about 90% of their time at home, where the highest risk of microplastic exposure in humans is found" (20). A study was conducted to determine how much microplastics were detected in common household dust deposits. Dust from 32 homes were collected, and 39% of the dust residue was, in fact, microplastic fibers. Chemicals that attach to microplastics settle in household dust particles. These chemicals cause damage to human DNA, with the potential to cause cancer. Dust deposits in the home can increase by up to 6000 or more microfibers per square meter every day; this number is doubled in carpeted homes. A quarter of household dust particles are small enough to be inhaled, along with whatever toxins that are attached to them. Children under the age of 6 are at the greatest risk for microplastic inhalation because of their small body size, higher breathing rates, close contact with the floor, and their tendency to touch their mouths and face after touching dusty, contaminated surfaces (20). Microplastics have been recently discovered in stool samples of adults and babies, as well as in the lung tissues and blood of living people (11, 12 and 13). Plastic items that are responsible for exposure of microplastics in infants are related to teethers, plastic toys, feeding bottles, and eating utensils (13). "Babies that are fed with plastic bottles swallow millions of microplastics a day" —*Guardian News and Media. (2022, March 24). Microplastics found in human blood for first time.* Microplastics have also been discovered in the placentas of pregnant women, which pass through the heart, lungs, and brain of their unborn baby. Human exposure to microplastics has become unavoidable (11). Various food items have been found to directly contain microplastics, the most common being, milk, honey, sugar, table salt, tap water, frozen meats, and seafood. Studies confirm that plastic food packaging is toxic to both the health of consumers, and the environment (18).

Microplastics that are found in tap water, have also been found to carry disease spreading organisms. Various United Nations Countries had their tap water tested, and 83% of the samples contained plastic fibers (1). Lung tissue samples were collected from 13, pre-surgery, living patients, and microplastics were detected in 11 samples. The plastic particles found were directly linked to the use of plastic packaging, and water bottles. Another study conducted in 1998 on lung cancer patients in the United States found both plastic and cotton fibers in the samples. Additionally, wearing plastic face masks also exposes people to microplastic inhalation. In March 2022, microplastics were found in human blood samples, and plastic particles travelling through the body demonstrated that those particles potentially get lodged in organ tissues (11). Microplastics were present in 80% of human blood samples tested. Microplastics that latch onto red blood cells reduce oxygen transport through the body, causing the contamination to pass through vital organs. The Earth has become completely contaminated with microplastics, with its presence found in the deepest oceans and even on top of Mount Everest (12). The most concerning component of this matter is that research is just starting to be conducted on what the consequences of so much plastic waste in the environment means for our health, and understanding the level of damage it has caused for each ecosystem on Earth. It is alarming that we know so little about the consequences linked to a product that is literally found everywhere, used every day, and even moving through our bodies right now. It is evident that action must be taken as soon as possible to reduce the world's plastic use, and production. Products designed for children should be made from plastic free materials in an attempt to reduce exposure of microplastics in children (13). Another way to decrease the risks for exposure to microplastics within the home, would be to replace carpeted floors with hard flooring, vacuuming carpeted areas on a weekly basis (20), and dusting surfaces.

The products we use in our everyday lives should be reassessed, and alternative materials for consumer goods should be implemented in order to replace plastic, and its rapid accumulation in landfills.

Photo Credit: *Here are how many baby bottles you need to buy.* CNET. (n.d.). Retrieved May 5, 2023, from https://www.cnet.com/health/parenting/how-many-baby-bottles-you-need-to-buy/

Chapter 6
The Plastic on My Plate

The flaking of microplastics into food and drinks is influenced by temperature, such as hot and cold. For example, frozen foods that are stored in plastic bags or hot food served on a plastic dish. Another point of microplastic ingestion is from warming food in the microwave using a plastic dish, along with the presence of microplastics being found in tap water (1), commercial food packaging are a few direct sources that expose people to microplastic contamination. Plastic dishes, and containers flake contaminants into the drinks and food they contain, including the food packaged and sold in the grocery store (18). Let's explore how the rest of our meal, and food sources encounter plastic contamination. Microplastics have been detected in the meat, milk, and blood of farm animals used as a common food source producing contaminated beef, pork, and milk products. A study conducted in the Netherlands found microplastics in every blood sample tested from 24 animals: 12 pigs and 12 cows (10). It was also confirmed that microplastics were present in all samples of animal pellet feed. Once microplastics are in the body, they cause damage to human cells. Current recycling methods include shredding waste food that is still packaged in plastic, and turning it into animal feed that contains "plastic in every scoop". —*Guardian News and Media. (2018, December 15). Legal plastic content in animal feed could harm human health, experts warn.* The cause for contamination in farm animals was a result of ingestion of microplastics through either feed that was stored in plastic packaging or by directly ingesting shredded pieces of plastic present in animal feed pellets.

Photo Credit: Guardian News and Media. (2018, December 15). *Legal plastic content in animal feed could harm human health, experts warn*. The Guardian. Retrieved May 6, 2023, from

https://www.theguardian.com/environment/2018/dec/15/legal-plastic-content-in-animal-feed-could-harm-human-health-experts-warn

Manufacturers are aware of the recycling processes that cause the presence of microplastics in animal and human food products, but the levels are considered within legal limits (9). However, there seems to be no transparency between manufacturers and the general public's knowledge in regards to the food people are consuming and how it may impact their health. If you find this appalling, consider the fact that we constantly contribute to this undesirable way of things every day, literally eating fragments of our own garbage and getting animals to eat it too because of our wasteful behaviors with toxic items, and chemicals that remain in the environment for hundreds of years. This is due to the lack of a better option for waste management for products that are not biodegradable, used briefly, discarded, then buried in a landfill leaching into soils and groundwater. Looking at it from this perspective, doesn't it encourage reevaluation of the type of waste we are producing in our daily lives? After all, we have become surrounded by it; it's even on our plate, a portion in every meal. The waste generated by the global population has entered every ecosystem on Earth, from the soils we grow our vegetables in, water in our irrigation systems, our tap water, to the cows and pigs on the farm set to be butchered for consumption. Banning plastic bags and using paper straws is a very small-scale adjustment to a much larger problem. At this point, it is getting harder to deny the harmful impact that man-made products continue to have on wildlife, the environment, and our own health. The main culprit for generating tons of plastic waste that accumulates and overwhelms landfill sites causing contamination, is the mass manufacturing of low-quality products that break easily, and are disposed of after a short period of use, are not biodegradable, and made with toxic chemicals. Consumer products that are meant to be reused over and over because they last a long time, but we use them in a disposable manner, like Tupperware that gets grimy from leftovers after a couple uses, lids get lost and mismatched, then they end up in the landfill for decades. In order to put an end to this issue, there must be a complete overhaul of consumer products, and food packaging. Outdated ideas about climate change issues being a problem for future generations must be abolished; this is a problem we are dealing with right now, and it's a big one. The fact that research is just emerging, and microplastics are not visible to the naked eye makes it difficult to raise concern on this issue. However, because it has entered every environment on the planet, makes this an issue that can no longer be avoided. We must not only make changes in the way we live and the products we use, but also conduct the necessary research required to see what health issues people might be experiencing due to the amount of toxic pollution we have generated through plastic use and production over the years, and how we can reduce those impacts. Source 3—Plastic Soup Foundation's article, "How Plastic has Entered the Food Chain" (2020) states that animals that excrete swallowed plastic may actually cleanse their bodies because toxins in the body have attached themselves to the plastic. I fear that statements like this give people a false sense of security, intended to change a readers' sense of reasoning, misleading them into thinking that something that is bad for them might actually be good, when it's not. Points discussed in this literature and others, confirmed that toxins and contaminants that are attached to microplastics also enter the human body in this way (20).

Chapter 7
Non-Toxic Alternatives

In regards to an alternative material that should be acknowledged and implemented on a wider scale across the world in the attempt to reduce plastic waste, global emissions, and the impact of climate change, the material that stood out above anything else to me, because of its many benefits was industrial hemp. Industrial hemp has been used to make items such as: "environmentally friendly fuel", ink, mulch, paper, carpet, and batteries that outperform our current energy storing devices. Hemp has also been used in making cosmetic make up, nail polish, water resistant clothing, lotion, baby diapers, replacement for plastic garbage and shopping bags, animal food, canvas, paint, varnish, shampoo, and sneakers. Hemp seeds have the ability to produce milk that is rich in Vitamins A, E, D, B12, and folic acid, it also makes a butter that is rich in fiber (7). Hemp is a natural product which can be used to make consumer products that are 5 times stiffer, stronger than, and just as durable as regular plastic (2). Hemp products have amazing potential to replace many common plastic items used today that contribute to global health concerns for people and wildlife, overwhelming landfills worldwide. The beneficial aspects of using hemp as a plastic alternative is that it is safe for the environment, and our body. Hemp skin care products have been tested and said to improve skin by reducing acne and slowing the ageing process when used in shampoos and lotions. It is rich in vitamins when consumed, and hemp is a completely renewable and sustainable resource. Batteries that are used today are extremely harmful to the environment; it is a hazardous waste product, which is almost never disposed of in the appropriate manner. Hemp batteries can help us resolve this issue, by reducing, and preventing further harm to the environment, wildlife species, and humans (7). Incorporating the transition to the use of hemp products instead of plastic, and other harmful building materials may help us get the results we wish for in achieving a sustainable future for the planet.

Chapter 8
The Plant as Mighty as An Oak

Industrial Hemp has the potential to replace many consumer products and building materials that are responsible for doing the most harm to the environment. This is because it produces plant-based products that are non-toxic, biodegradable, and does not generate harmful emissions from its use (28). Considering this alternative solution would be better for the environment and pose less risk to plant, animal, and human health. Practices like laying concrete for building foundations, sidewalks, and roadways, deteriorate, and compact soils with toxic chemicals. Not only are we preventing the Earth from breathing by coating top soils with toxic chemicals like the ones present in cement and using them to build structures, but these harmful contaminants become airborne during building demolition (29), raising concern regarding air quality. The materials currently used for structural development and road access are poisonous for human health, as they pollute various ecosystems. This is a compelling reason why the use of alternative materials should be a global movement in order to reduce exposure to these chemicals. Opportunities to implement the use of industrial hemp include making hemp plastic, fuel, and alternatives for structural building materials like: lumber, concrete, rope, firewood, and other timber products. The list of possibilities go on, and on. Products like hempwood can greatly reduce rates of clear-cut logging caused by the high demand for timber products, allowing tree populations to recover naturally after years of rapid deforestation. Alternative wood products made from hemp fiber are as durable as Oak wood (16), making hemp "The Plant As Mighty As An Oak". With the legalization of marijuana in Canada, it would be a profitable economic move to establish hemp-product manufacturing within the country, and around the globe in an attempt to put an end to the use of, and accumulation of garbage produced by plastic products. Industrial hemp products are made from the stalk fibers, and the seeds of the plant, while the flower is used for medicinal purposes or leisure use. All parts of the plant can be used, but fibers and seeds of the plant are the most desired; from any species of hemp plant (21) in order to make hemp products. An industrial hemp crop produces fiber or seeds that can be used to make hemp products like paper, rope, fuel, wood and concrete alternatives, oil and chemical absorption products, vehicle parts, clothes, sunscreen, paint, shoes, animal bedding, and kitty litter. Home growers and the general public would be able to contribute by providing hemp fiber and seeds produced by legally growing hemp from home. This would also reduce the number of large agricultural properties required for growing hemp crops by allowing the general public to assist, because industrial hemp can successfully be grown in raised garden beds. Industrial hemp products do not cause intoxication or off-gassing into homes from its use as a building material or from burning (15). Hemp building products can also remove carbon from the surrounding environment, which is a complete reversal of the roles of our current building construction practices, which are the driving forces for toxic emissions of pollutants into the atmosphere. Implementing the use of industrial hemp timber products will also help reduce stress on tree populations, reducing the impact of deforestation that has resulted in habitat loss for many wildlife species. Logging has also put wild salmon populations at risk by reducing tree coverage surrounding natural waterbodies allowing for more direct sunlight to increase the temperature of open waters. Growing industrial hemp suppresses weed growth, and repels pests, which eliminates the need for heavy use of pesticides, and herbicides that create toxic runoff into natural water sources and soils, killing birds and insects that are essential to natural ecosystems (2). Believe it or not, insects and birds play an important role in the world. Many land insects like snails are essential for soil formation, and birds are pollinators that assist in plant species diversity as they transport, and disperse seeds throughout the environment. Speaking of pollinators, honey bees have also been affected by microplastics in the environment. The same way that bees collect pollen from plants with the small hairs on their bodies, they have now been found to be collecting particles of airborne microplastics (19), along with being another casualty of pesticide and herbicide poisoning. Insects are essential to soil porosity, making tiny air pockets as they move through soils, allowing better flow of nutrients and water, required for richer, healthier, soils with higher nutrient content, suitable for growing crops. Soil organisms also break down and decompose leaf litter dropped across the forest floor in autumn. Many of our current practices cause soil compaction, such as running heavy equipment that reduces pore space in the soils, restricting water flow, and creating a habitat that is unlivable for soil organisms. Insects and soil organisms are essential to maintaining healthy soil ecosystems that support vegetation.

Chapter 9
A Revolution with Hemp Plastic

A step in the right direction. Implementing the use of hemp based plastic products can drastically transform the way that plastic waste contaminates our environment on a daily basis. Hemp plastic is a plant-based material that decomposes after use without producing carbon dioxide emissions, and is not a product of fossil fuels. Hemp plastic is flexible, strong, durable, non-toxic, lighter weight, denser and cheaper than current plastic products. One thing to take into consideration is that hemp plastic degrades within six months (26). However, the use of this product would be ideal for short-term use products like packaging for lunch foods that are readily sold in grocery stores on a daily basis, baked goods, packaged food in general has a limited shelf life with an expiration date, so making the switch from plastic manufactured with harmful chemicals to plant-based hemp plastic could also reduce microplastic ingestion caused by contamination from food packaging. By changing the chemically hazardous materials currently used to make plastic products, and switching to biodegradable, earth friendly alternatives like hemp, will have a positive impact on minimizing how long waste stays in the environment after it is discarded, while preventing run off of toxic chemicals from harmful products that can be replaced with industrial hemp based alternatives. The use of industrial hemp for automotive parts was proposed and implemented in 1941 by Henry Ford, who constructed a vehicle made from hemp materials that could be fueled by vegetable or hemp oil and was demonstrated to be "ten times stronger than steel". —*Baxter, D. (2022, June 20). Hemp plastic: 5 advantages for biodegradable products. Plant Switch.* Proposal of the hemp vehicle occurred during the same time vehicles running on fossil fuels were becoming the industrial standard, so the idea of manufacturing hemp vehicles got overpowered, and pushed aside. As a test of strength, Henry Ford struck his hemp vehicle with an axe which failed to dent or damage the vehicle (2). In hindsight, if the powers that be given Henry Ford's idea a chance to take off when he presented it, we probably would not be in the threatening climate change predicament we find ourselves in today. I recognize in writing this literature, I am facing a similar predicament: It's hard to change the minds of people that are stuck in the outdated ways of the past, regardless of how it may condemn future generations. This is especially true for those that have benefited financially from the use of fossil fuels, and have used it as leverage to control the general public, and other countries' through reliance on transportation, and the need for home heating. They raise price at the gas pumps without offering a glimpse into the future regarding fossil fuels, while avoiding any recognition of the available alternatives thought up by brilliant minds over the years. Voices silenced in competition with decision makers that are secure in knowing that gas prices can be raised as high as inflation will allow, while people have no other choice than to accommodate rising gas prices. This includes the discovery of vehicles fueled by water. The pursuit of and dependence on fossil fuels have led to wars between countries, and is still being used as a control tactic over the general public. There seems to be an indication that greenhouse gas emissions, produced by carbon dioxide from vehicle exhaust, may have people needing to give up their vehicles or choose other methods of transportation in order to decrease the risk of climate change. The use of biofuels and non-toxic batteries, with vehicle panels molded from a hemp composite, can allow for continued use of motor vehicles that are redesigned to not produce harmful emissions that deplete the ozone layer, and reduce air quality across the planet. Another issue is the accumulation of abandoned, broken-down vehicles, which contribute to junk yards filled with metals and hazardous waste fluids like coolants, oils and battery acid that do not break down and contaminate the surrounding environment for years. The most recent idea for implementing the use of electric vehicles to replace fossil fuels also comes with the consequence of increased mining activity for lithium that will greatly increase harmful practices that result in further environmental degradation.

Chapter 10
Effects of Using Concrete

Harmful construction materials and practices, like laying concrete for building foundations, sidewalks and roadways, deteriorate, erode, compact soils, and contaminate water sources. Roadway developments are one of the main causes for interference with fish migration routes, preventing fish species from making their way back to essential spawning grounds causing a decrease in fish populations. Even with culverts installed under roadways in an attempt to salvage fish migration routes, access can easily be cut off by accumulation of woody debris that interferes with water levels, ultimately drying up water sources completely over time. If culverts are not regularly maintained, and inspected, they can create a dead end for fish when they become perched after installation, preventing access to water sources that are important for fish populations, biodiversity and conservation.

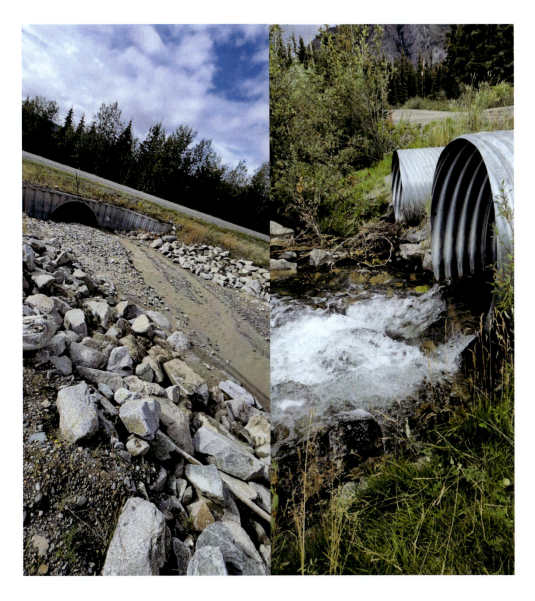

Roadway, commercial, and residential developments should be well thought out before developing, taking into consideration which animal species may be affected. I've witnessed a major increase of unnecessary road developments, like an overabundance of traffic circles, which involve clear cutting of surrounding trees minimizing wildlife habitat and corridors, creating more potential for human-wildlife conflicts. Dust created during building demolition creates air pollution that is toxic to human health. The current building materials used in construction are hazardous to the environment and contribute to climate change, also putting the handler of the substance at risk of exposure to chemicals that can damage the respiratory tract, and create various other toxic reactions upon contact (29). People are exposed to these chemicals while spending time indoors, inhaling flame retardants, and other toxic chemicals present in carpets and other building materials.

Photo Credit: Olivier DUPORT-hemp block ep 15 and wood frame

Hempcrete is an alternative to concrete made with the woody core of the industrial hemp plant, called hemp hurd which is dried and broken into chips then mixed with a Lime binder and water. One unavoidable practice required for making Hempcrete is mining Lime (24). However, this is a common practice already used in order to treat tailings ponds for acid mine drainage in the Mining Industry. The Lime binder combines very well with the industrial hemp plant because it is silica rich, this component is what makes Hempcrete durable. In structures built with Hempcrete, the Lime binder prevents mold, repels pests, and is resistant to fire. Hempcrete can be used for slab, roof, and wall insulation with pour in, tilt up panel placement. Hempcrete can maintain quality in humid conditions, regulates moisture, and is 20X lighter than concrete. Structures built with hempcrete still require steel framing for load bearing support, but are durable enough to still be standing 100 years later, providing a family home for generations. The low density of Hempcrete makes it resistant to cracking caused by movement, this would benefit regions prone to earthquakes, providing maximum strength and no off gassing in the home. Manufacturing Hempcrete absorbs carbon and removes toxins from the atmosphere, the surrounding environment, and continues to do so during building construction, maintenance and operation (24).

Chapter 11
Industrial Hemp Cutting Down on Deforestation

An alternative lumber product that can be manufactured from using industrial hemp is hempwood, which can be burned for heat, used as flooring, making furniture, and particle boards for construction. Hempwood is a good thermal conductor, has high porosity, burns and insulates just as good as natural wood for heat. Firewood for home heating puts trees in high demand, so this alternative option can help relieve the demand on tree populations. Industrial hemp does not cause intoxication from being used or burned. Hempwood products are made from hemp fibers held together with soy-based adhesives, and do not emit any toxic chemicals, and has resistance to pests and weeds. Hempwood provides stability that is less likely to twist and warp, and it is easily repaired, refinished, sanded, and reused. Trees take a very long time to grow into a usable size for timber products and are harvested soon after maturity. This is why it is important to look to alternative wood products so we can allow the trees to recover naturally, after decades of rapid forest depletion (16). Implementing the use of hemp as a wood alternative would be extremely productive because it can be regenerated in 6-month intervals, from harvest to regrowth, and produces four times more paper per acre than trees. Deforestation of wildlife habitat for timber products, human developments, use of herbicides and pesticides in agriculture have literally left wildlife species with nowhere to go. We keep expanding into every natural habitat available leaving it contaminated and unlivable for most species, even our own. The hemp plant has fast growth rates, growing 4 meters high in only 3 months, and can be harvested every 120 days (15). With a high harvest interval, as always, care must be taken not to compact soils; they require less fertilization, less water, and leaves soils in a healthier state that supports crop rotation. The Industrial Hemp plant is sown October through March. Plant growth naturally suppresses weeds. The biggest concern with growing Industrial Hemp is birds stripping the plants of seeds. As soon as birds begin stripping seeds from the crop, it must be harvested immediately. Two hundred and fifty plants per square meter would be required for fiber production. Typical farming equipment may be required for a large-scale crops including tractors, balers, and a dry storage facility for fibers. Growing industrial hemp has water supply and light requirements during the growth period. Additional equipment may include an irrigation system, sickle bar mowers, and hay swathers. Hemp fiber comes from the stem of the plant, not the flower. This makes it a good opportunity to include home growers in the process of manufacturing. In home growing operations of hemp, it is usually the flower that is most commonly used for medicinal and recreational purposes, and the stems and fibers of the plant are not being utilized. Therefore, having a system where people can contribute and get paid for their unused or discarded hemp fibers and seeds, that can be used in manufacturing industrial hemp products, would help reduce the number of big properties required for growing hemp. With legalization of marijuana in Canada, the hemp flower is already being grown, harvested, and sold to the public. This process could now include making use of every part of the plant so that new earth-friendly-hemp-based products can be manufactured and become the standard across the world, in order to put an end to the rapid accumulation of toxic waste. Giving the general public and manufacturers a new resource to focus on, where almost anyone can get involved, and actually do their part in battling climate change.

Chapter 12
Harm Reduction with Alternative Hemp Products

So, how can industrial hemp products improve our current consumer products? Industrial hemp is capable of replacing hazardous materials, like rope, where a lot of it ends up in the oceans from commercial fishing. Using hemp to make rope that replaces polyester and nylon rope will reduce harm to aquatic life, shorebirds, and humans that consume seafood. Rope and fishing nets are the leading cause for entanglement, and strangulation of wildlife, causing death in most cases. Birds eat them and build their nests with these fibers. Hemp alternatives can reduce these risks as they are plant-based, made without harmful chemicals, and it degrades over time, meaning that fragments that do inevitably end up in natural water sources will naturally decompose. Hemp has also been used to make lotions, cosmetics, nail polish, shampoo, and make-up (7). Current products are labelled with a list of chemicals used to make them. It makes you wonder what side effects could be related to using products filled with chemicals being applied to your skin, hair, face, and nails. Cosmetic products are absorbed into your body through your skin, which is concerning, especially when applying glues for eyelash extensions, eye shadow and foundations. My concern is that applying chemicals to your face and so close to your eyes could impact your vision and overall health with extended use of these products. Over the years, many shampoos have been recalled over the years for causing hair loss and other chemical reactions. Ingredients contained in cosmetics are often obtained in an unethical manner, a product of deforestation creating loss of wildlife habitat, especially those from unique tropical rain forest ecosystems that are not easily regenerated. Old growth forests have been over harvested at a devastating rate. That is why it is essential that we start using great products like Hempwood so that tree populations can recover from decades of overharvest. By using building materials like Hempcrete and hempwood, along with hemp made carpets, flooring, and particle boards, construction companies can build structures that reduce exposure to toxins while spending time indoors. Fuel is another major source for contamination in the environment, and dependency on fossil fuels has rapidly depleted air quality on Earth, and has created a hole in the ozone layer. This depletion makes people more prone to harm from the sun's UV rays, causing skin cancer, and having temperatures rise to critical levels that exceed optimal temperatures that sustain most living organisms on the planet. Warmer climates have experienced an increase of fatalities due to increasing temperatures in those regions. Making biofuels from hemp are better for the environment because hemp requires less water, about 10–15 inches per season, and is able to be successfully grown almost anywhere. The use of hemp-made biofuels will allow for more food production because other bio fuel oils are obtained from sacrificing edible crops. Hemp can produce biodiesel, and methanol/ethanol type fuels that are faster to produce, and we wouldn't have to worry about harmful air pollution. With rising populations, more common items that overflow from landfills are baby diapers, and feminine pads. As times have changed, people are less attracted to the idea of using reusable diapers, which requires handling fecal matter, and washing waste products from clothing fibers. In the past, Indigenous people used to make diapers out of moss, which also had properties that prevent diaper rash because the plant is good at retaining moisture. Industrial hemp could also be used to replace plastic baby diapers, reducing tons of harmful waste produced on a daily basis (7). Earth-friendly products like reusable pads for feminine hygiene products are already available on the market from select earth savvy vendors.

Chapter 13
A Wider Perspective

We are all well aware of the climate change crisis, with an increase in natural disasters lurking around every corner. Sitting back and continuing on with the current products and practices we use today will just accelerate the problem to an irreversible state of disaster.

Once the general public becomes aware of this, the issue can no longer be avoided, and people will want to know what they can do to help. Just because we have become comfortable in the way things are currently being done, and have gotten used to this way of living, generating excess amounts of garbage every day, doesn't mean that it's right! It's self-destructive. As the saying goes, "If you do what you've always done, you'll get what you've always got." – Henry Ford. Don't wait for the people that are benefiting financially to be the ones to speak up for change. With or without the approval of those contributing to the problem, the time for change is now. I assure you that manufacturers will not be the ones admitting to any fault or taking any accountability for their harmful practices. People do not like to admit when they are wrong, especially when they can get away with it, and have been for decades. It's up to the people that actually care about the planet, having clean drinking water, having a world that is suitable for future generations, and wildlife organisms that are essential to functioning ecosystems across the planet. Products just aren't made the way they used to be. Retailers, consumer product companies, and their manufacturers rely on the fact that their product will break easily or need regular maintenance which keeps the consumer coming back buying the same product to replace the last one. It's a ridiculous cycle with a heavy cost for the environment. Another issue regarding a sensitive subject; being someone who has dealt with the loss of many loved ones having passed away, during gatherings, memorial services or celebrations many people find comfort in releasing lanterns, and balloons into the sky to acknowledge their loved one. Where do you think those balloons go? Up into the heavens? Into outer space? No! They get swept away by wind currents, which are almost always drawn to oceans, and other water sources. The balloons pop and accumulate in the oceans for birds, sea turtles, and other aquatic mammals to eat, starve, from no nutritional benefit, and get strangled or choked by the ribbons attached to the plastic waste caused by those sentimental gestures of releasing balloons into the sky. This is another prime example of choosing comfort over consequence. Every single holiday, every year, parents are pressured into buying all the junk associated with whatever holiday it is; noise makers, funny glasses for St. Patrick's Day, and New Year's, Mardi gras beads, plastic Easter eggs. Halloween costumes, chocolates, and candies individually wrapped in plastic, then sold within another bag of plastic, and some items packed with multiple layers of plastic wrapping for one small item. It's outrageous. We do this every holiday as a testament of our love for children, which also brings stress and guilt to low-income households that struggle to meet the demands of society, having to keep up with appearances, and feeling less than if they can't afford Valentine's Day cards for everyone in their child's classroom or daycare, then have to do it all over again the next year. The point is that we can still honor our loved ones in memory in other ways, and we can still show our children that we love them without having to buy so much plastic, disposable junk that just sits in the landfill after being used for short term gratification. If we want to continue these practices, then it is essential that we take action in changing what those products are made from.

Photo Credit: *{{productdata.name}}*. 21703371–BostBest Shopping Mall. (n.d.). Retrieved May 6, 2023, from https://salersov.xyz/product_details/21703371.html

Chapter 14
How Can the Average Joe Make a Difference?

In order to make change that will help the environment and relieve the pressure of rising temperatures due to climate change and melting permafrost, there must be a surge of effort put in around the globe to create change that ensures a greener future for all beings. Ways that the general public can help reduce waste is by recycling clothing; old, torn clothes usually get thrown in the garbage, but the fibers of damaged clothing can be repurposed if you donate those items to your local recycling center, and better-quality items can be donated to those in need. It takes approximately 1800 gallons of water to make one pair of blue jeans from cotton, and 400 gallons for one t-shirt; this only includes making the clothing, not the water required for every wash (6). The dye present in one pair of blue jeans has the potential to dye an entire lake or pond if discarded by a water source, something to keep in mind when taking off layers at the beach. Another way to reduce waste, and harmful emissions is to repurpose items, donate unwanted or unused possessions, and compost spoiled food. Leftovers and organic matter like banana peels, apple cores, and yard clippings or garden waste emit carbon into the atmosphere when discarded, and organic food decomposes in the landfill. Composting food is a messy job, but it makes a big difference for the planet in terms of greenhouse gas emissions. Also, keep in mind that composted foods contained in "organic" recycling bags are still just another plastic bag that gets shredded along with compost foods then used to make organic soils that contain microplastics, just like the products we are feeding livestock derived from common recycling practices; everything prepared for consumption is served with a grain of plastic. Another important practice is making an effort to properly dispose of hazardous waste, saving batteries, oils, coolants, toner cartridges, aerosol cans etc., until the local landfill hosts a hazardous waste disposal day, which sadly only occurs once or twice a year in most places. Reusing holiday decorations, and bringing all broken electronics to an e-waste disposal center, this includes damaged cords, electric toothbrushes, old TVs, laptops, vacuum cleaners, fans, heaters, or anything with an electrical cord attached to it. These items must be disposed of properly so they don't contaminate the environment, accompanied by active remediation of already contaminated areas caused by hazardous waste. I think the holiday we should be glorifying the most is Earth Day, and that people should feel obligated to pick up trash in their neighborhood or wherever they find it, more often than just over lunch hour one day a year. These are ways that we can work towards caring more deeply for the environment, and cleaning up the mess we've already made as a species. Humans are the greatest abuser of our natural resources here on Earth, and it's time we start respecting the land we live on, making wiser choices, respecting wildlife, and changing the way we do things all together. Implementing the use of industrial hemp products has the potential to make a great impact that can halt the progress of climate change. We can't let the people who have gotten rich off the current practices bully us into staying stagnant, preventing us from shifting to a new direction, because their bank account balance comes first before the health of this planet or any concern for what future generations will have to deal with.

Chapter 15
Legalized Growing of Hemp

Aleks-Hemp harvesting in France

Legally growing hemp in Canada requires Government issued licensing and permits that must be renewed every year for a license, and every 3 months for permits. All application forms, general information, and requirements are listed on the Government of Canada website for those who are interested in growing hemp for medical, and non-medical purposes. Licenses expire on the last day of December, and applications are accepted in November for the next growing season. After obtaining a license and permit to grow cannabis, the license holder then has the right to import and export industrial hemp with the appropriate permits in place for that purpose. They also have the right to produce, sell, transport, possess, and deliver industrial hemp legally. There are activities that can be done by those who do not hold a license for growing cannabis, which includes growing non-viable cannabis seeds, and using fibers, and bare stalks that are without leaves, flowers, branches or seeds, then making use of the fibers to make hemp-based products. Growing a maximum of 4 plants per household, and producing approximately "30 grams of non-medical personally grown cannabis to use, share with, but not sell to anyone of legal age" —*Canada, H. (2018, November 7). Government of Canada.* When you obtain a cultivating license, and register yourself with Health Canada for growing cannabis for medical purposes, with compliance to regulations you can arrange a production limit during your registration then proceed to grow cannabis within that limit from legally sourced seeds, which makes them viable (4). The plant's short growth time from planting to maturity makes it ideal for fiber production used to make consumer products, with mature fibers ready to harvest within 85–120 days (3). Now that we know the difference between modest personal growing of cannabis compared to requirements for larger growing operations, both small-, and large-scale cannabis farming operations can have an opportunity to assist with contributing fibers for industrial hemp products. Once it becomes mainstream common knowledge about how industrial hemp could drastically impact the fight against climate change, how could we not support implementing the use of hemp products worldwide? It's nice to see that progress is being made in the hemp industry, but that progress needs to be accelerated, because we can't keep pumping the planet full of plastic like we do every day. As a parent, I care about what kind of world my children will be living in, I care about their future, and take into consideration what cultural practices and food sources that have been lost over time from rapidly declining wildlife populations. As a Renewable Resource Management graduate, I care about the fate of this planet, and every plant, animal, insect and person who lives here, including the outdated thinkers. However, it's time for them to step aside, allowing real action to take place. We need to reduce anthropogenic threats to the environment and manufacture products that are not threatening to our health, and poisoning the environment.

Chapter 16
Conclusion

Our beautiful, lush planet has really taken a beating from the human race. Wildlife and every natural ecosystem has suffered as a result from excess contamination caused by outdated practices and the low-quality plastic garbage that we mass produce. If this planet stands a fighting chance for the future, change has to be made now, not in 10 to 20 years while we continue the same harmful practices, and turn a blind eye to a rapidly growing catastrophe. The potential for industrial hemp to improve our current practices, and environmental state has been dormant, but now is the time to allow full release of its potential for a better, more sustainable future. Damage to soils caused by rapid development of human built structures, roads, and heavy agricultural impact has resulted in low nutrient soils that become more difficult to produce healthy crops or support natural ecosystems. Every single ecosystem on this planet serves an important function, and it is imperative that we nurture, and care for every single one of them; they are all connected, the soils, water, air, insects, birds, and wildlife. Every species is essential to managing homeostasis in nature; the quality of one ecosystem affects the quality of another. We divide ourselves into different countries across the globe, fighting over natural resources, differences in race, and religion, fighting for power fueled by greed, when in reality we are all connected, we are one, we are in this together, and we only have one planet. World wars have nations fighting against each other, bombing parts of the world, inflicting cultural genocide, killing people, and destroying the planet over resources and the need to be right, when what is actually needed is to be working together in finding a global solution that ensures sustaining life here on earth. We all live on the same planet; a country's border doesn't change that. Threats of nuclear bombing, with excessive mining of natural resources ultimately condemns every living thing on Earth, for what? A pissing contest between politicians? Systemic racism? Forced agendas fueled by those who will profit financially; we are all in this together, but for how long? That is up to us and how we choose to move forward from here. We must make an effort to evolve as a species, and move beyond using violence as a control tactic when someone with power, financial resources, and social status doesn't get their way. When we stand together, and come to appreciate what each unique being has to offer, then we can really help the world thrive as a whole. This includes every bee that comes to visit your garden, when we value, and actually recognize how important they are as pollinators, we would step back, and let a bee, be a bee, not go running to the store for a bottle of insecticide. Insects and soil organisms are essential for pollinating medicinal wild plants that are often overlooked for their healing benefits even while being found in our own backyards.

Bird species are also essential for pollination, and should be protected. However, bird populations continue to decline by the billions every year from deaths caused by house cats, which are an introduced species, window collisions, and poisoning from herbicides and insecticides. Aquatic and land insects in their larval stages, and one of the most fascinating things I've learned is that macro-invertebrates are the most essential part of any water ecosystem, even more important than fish, because they improve water quality by filtering out waste. People think that bugs are pests that must be extinguished, and that they don't matter, but I assure you they do. Dragonflies, for example go through a great transformation; they begin life in the water before they take to the land and begin to fly. I feel like we can take a lesson from this great transformation experienced by butterflies and dragonflies, and the lesson I am referring to is that life can be one way for a long time, and it may seem okay, until one day you transform into something completely different that takes you to incredible heights that you've never imagined.

Plants and animals have their own natural order and function that play an important role in maintaining balance in nature. Seemingly insignificant things are actually extremely important, beyond the comprehension of the average person. Trees in a forested area are actually connected to one another as well. Through the network of fungi mycelium underneath the surface of Earth, they can detect harm, and share nutrients with each other with the presence of fungi. This large network beneath the tree community is invisible from the surface, just like how microplastics have entered the food chain, our lungs, and bodies. What is clearly visible, is the fact that plastic waste has gotten out of control, and if we continue to mass produce harmful products like plastic, and use it every day, things will continue to get worse for everyone, and everything on Earth. It's time to reevaluate our current practices, our attitudes, and toxic behaviors regarding the world around us. In a busy world, people have lost touch with humanity, distracted from getting in touch with nature. We're too busy trying to make a living dealing with the stress of everyday life. With health issues on the rise, seldom do people just stop, take a breath, and make the time to get out and enjoy nature, and soak in all of its beauty. Admiring a sunrise, sunset, the glow of the full moon, the call of seabirds against crashing waves, the gentle flow of water in a stream, or getting a glimpse of a unique wildlife species – one of the most healing practices is being out in nature, and taking notice of all the animal species that you share a home with in your local region. I hope that the quality of those experiences are maintained for future generations, starting with taking better care of Mother Nature. She needs us now more than ever. By implementing global use of industrial hemp-based products, we can make huge progress in our battle against climate change, and change how the products we mass produce impact the environment, ensuring a more promising future for everyone. The problem these days is when there is an appealing natural habitat like forested areas with abundant resources, the first thought is, what kind of establishment would look good here? Or what resources can we extract, leaving the area completely depleted in exchange for economic gain. I have witnessed many transformations in my own local region over the years: completely wooded areas that have been cleared and converted into large residential neighborhoods, ponds that have dried up, increase of wildfires, mountains that used to have yearlong snow cover, now melting, exposing mountain tops, creating excess water drainage from mountain ice and snow melt that loosens up soils creating landslides and melting permafrost. Developments continue in sensitive areas with no regard for the consequences. I think the main priority now should be reducing our carbon footprint by implementing wide-scale use of industrial hemp products, especially in an attempt to remove plastic from the food chain, and from being the side dish you get with every meal.

Annotated Bibliography

Afrin, S., Uddin, M. K., & Rahman, M. M. (2020, November 25). Microplastics contamination in the soil from urban landfill site, Dhaka, Bangladesh. Heliyon, Vol. 6, issue 11, Retrieved April 15, 2022, from https://www.sciencedirect.com/science/article/pii/S2405844020324154

Baxter, D. (2022, June 20). Hemp plastic: 5 advantages for biodegradable products. Plant Switch. Retrieved April 24, 2023, from https://www.plantswitch.com/hemp-plastic/

Canada, H. (2018, November 7). Government of Canada. Canada.ca. Retrieved April 28, 2023, from https://www.canada.ca/en/health-canada/services/drugs-medication/cannabis/producing-selling-hemp/about-hemp-canada-hemp-industry/frequently-asked-questions.html#a5

Canada, H. (2022, October 11). Government of Canada. Canada.ca. Retrieved April 28, 2023, from https://www.canada.ca/en/health-canada/services/drugs-medication/cannabis/personal-use/growing-cannabis-home-safely.html#a1
Depositphotos. (2023, March 6). "plasticosis:" new disease in birds highlights dangers of microplastics. New Atlas. Retrieved April 28, 2023, from https://newatlas.com/biology/plasticosis-new-disease-microplastics-birds/

Frampton, K. (2017, November 30). Industrial water usage to produce these items: The71percent. The 71 Percent. Retrieved April 27, 2023, from https://www.the71percent.org/industrial-water-usage/

Garland, R. (2020, November 4). 25 things you didn't know are made from Hemp. Green Flower News. Retrieved April 30, 2023, from https://news.green-flower.com/25-things-you-didn-t-know-could-be-made-from-hemp/

(Website) —Green ammunition. Ammo and Bullet. (2020). Retrieved April 30, 2023, from https://www.ammoandbullet.com/green-ammunition/

(Website) —Guardian News and Media. (2018, December 15). Legal plastic content in animal feed could harm human health, experts warn. The Guardian. Retrieved February 21, 2023, from https://www.theguardian.com/environment/2018/dec/15/legal-plastic-content-in-animal-feed-could-harm-human-health-experts-warn

(Website) —Guardian News and Media. (2022, July 8). Microplastics detected in meat, milk and blood of farm animals. The Guardian. Retrieved February 22, 2023, from https://www.theguardian.com/environment/2022/jul/08/microplastics-detected-in-meat-milk-and-blood-of-farm-animals

(Website) – Guardian News and Media. (2022, April 6). Microplastics found deep in lungs of living people for first time. The Guardian. Retrieved April 13, 2022, from https://www.theguardian.com/environment/2022/apr/06/microplastics-found-deep-in-lungs-of-living-people-for-first-time

(Website) – Guardian News and Media. (2022, March 24). Microplastics found in human blood for first time. The Guardian. Retrieved March 27, 2022, from
https://www.theguardian.com/environment/2022/mar/24/microplastics-found-in-human-blood-for-first-time

(Website) – Guardian News and Media. (2021, September 22). More microplastics in babies' faeces than in adults'–study. The Guardian. Retrieved April 13, 2022, from
https://www.theguardian.com/science/2021/sep/22/more-microplastics-in-babies-faeces-than-in-adults-study

(Website) – Hemp. Green Flower News. Retrieved March 28, 2022, from https://news.green-flower.com/25-things-you-didn-t-know-could-be-made-from-hemp/

(Website) – Hempwood®. HempWood.com. (2023, April 13). Retrieved April 26, 2023, from
https://hempwood.com/

(Website) – Hempwood: The Sustainable Material Alternative to Wood! All House Related Solutions. (2021, May 11). Retrieved February 27, 2023, from https://gharpedia.com/blog/hempwood-the-alternative-to-wood/

(Website) – How plastic has entered the Food Chain. Plastic Soup Foundation. (2020, May 1). Retrieved April 15, 2022, from https://www.plasticsoupfoundation.org/en/plastic-problem/plastic-affect-animals/plastic-food-chain/

(Journal) – Jadhav, E. B., Sankhla, M. S., Bhat, R. A., & Bhagat, D. S. (2021, November 9). Microplastics from Food Packaging: An overview of human consumption, health threats, and alternative solutions. Environmental Nanotechnology, Monitoring & Management. Retrieved March 18, 2022, from
https://www.sciencedirect.com/science/article/abs/pii/S2215153221001835

(Website) – Kelly, M. (2021, May 24). Honeybees are accumulating airborne microplastics on their bodies. Environment. Retrieved April 24, 2023, from
https://www.nationalgeographic.com/environment/article/honeybees-are-accumulating-airborne-microplastics-on-their-bodies

(Journal) – Mark Patrick Taylor Professor of Environmental Science and Human Health, Neda Sharifi Soltani Academic Casual, & Scott P. Wilson Macquarie University. (2022, March 28). We're all ingesting microplastics at home, and these might be toxic for our health. here are some tips to reduce your risk. The Conversation. Retrieved April 15, 2022, from https://theconversation.com/were-all-ingesting-microplastics-at-home-and-these-might-be-toxic-for-our-health-here-are-some-tips-to-reduce-your-risk-159537#:~:text=Australians%20are%20eating%20and%20inhaling,in%20dust%20around%20the%20house.

(Website) – McMahon, A. (2022, January 23). 7 reasons hemp fuel is good for the environment. WAMA Underwear. Retrieved April 29, 2023, from https://wamaunderwear.com/blogs/news/hemp-fuel#:~:text=WHAT%20IS%20HEMP%20FUEL%3F,from%20the%20hemp%20plant%20stalk.

(Journal) – Microplastics. Wasser 3.0. (n.d.). Retrieved April 15, 2022, from
https://wasserdreinull.de/en/microplastics/

(Journal) – Microplastics and the impact of … - Institute of Physics. (n.d.). Retrieved April 16, 2022, from https://iopscience.iop.org/article/10.1088/1755-1315/528/1/012013

(Website) – Roberts, T. (2021, June 6). Building with hempcrete. Rise. Retrieved May 3, 2023, from https://www.buildwithrise.com/stories/building-with-hempcrete

(Website) – Sam TotoniJames FabisiakMartha Ann Terry, Totoni, S., Fabisiak, J., & Terry, M. A. (2022, December 7). Lead in hunted meat: Who's telling hunters and their families? EHN. Retrieved April 29, 2023, from https://www.ehn.org/lead-ammunition-in-meat-2645108170.html

(Website) – Sensi Seeds. (2020, April 30). Hemp plastic: What is it and how is it made? Sensi Seeds. Retrieved April 24, 2023, from https://sensiseeds.com/en/blog/hemp-plastic-what-is-it-and-how-is-it-made/

(Website) – Siossian, E. (2018, October 5). Satin Bowerbirds do a risky dance with plastic waste. ABC News. Retrieved April 28, 2023, from https://www.abc.net.au/news/2018-10-06/satin-bowerbirds-falling-victim-to-plastic-waste/10215078

(Website) – Vivek, V. (2023, April 21). How can hemp help to reduce deforestation: Hemp Foundation. Ukhi. Retrieved April 24, 2023, from
https://hempfoundation.net/how-can-hemp-fight-deforestation/#:~:text=Hemp%20requires%20very%20less%20or,polluting%20the%20other%20water%20bodies.

(Website) – Wikimedia Foundation. (2023, April

Environmental impact of concrete. Wikipedia. Retrieved April 26, 2023, from https://en.wikipedia.org/wiki/Environmental_impact_of_concrete